For Larry Kramer —
This black-humoured detour
in a '52 PICK-UP

With good recall

Peter

3/9/87
D.C.

ALSO BY PETER KLAPPERT
    Lugging Vegetables to Nantucket
    Circular Stairs, Distress in the Mirrors
    Non Sequitur O'Connor
    The Idiot Princess of the Last Dynasty

'52 PICK-UP

Scenes from **The Conspiracy**
A Documentary

A POEM IN 52 SCENES, 2 JOKERS, AND AN EXTRA ACE OF SPADES

PETER KLAPPERT

ORCHISES   1984   Washington

Library of Congress Cataloging in Publication Data

Klappert, Peter.
   '52 pick-up.
     I. Title.   II. Title: Fifty-two pick-up.
PS3561.L23A15   1984   811'.54   84–3245
ISBN 0-914061-02-X

Cover: detail from "Time to Bleed the Turkey" by Sheba Sharrow

Photo: H. E. Klappert

The author is grateful to the National Endowment for the Arts, The Millay Colony for the Arts, and The Virginia Center for the Creative Arts.

Published by Orchises Press; 4831 Alton Place, N.W.; Washington, D.C. 20016.

Manufactured in the United States of America
G6E4C2A.

'52 PICK-UP

picture	sound

Empty vacuum.	(Dictionary Voice:)
	In criminal law.
	A combination or
	confederacy between
	two or more
	persons formed for
	the purpose of committing by
	their joint efforts some
	unlawful or criminal act or
	some act which is innocent in
	itself but
Parturition & traumata:	becomes unlawful when
	done by the concerted actions of
	the conspirators or
vitamins	for the purpose of using criminal or
a e i o u,	unlawful means to
	the commission of an act not
	in itself unlawful. Or
marble sonnets	in other words

prose before swine.

newt music

(VO:)

Ladies And Gents, Our National Anthem

The Conspiracy asks each other to dance.

□□■□□

pump & circumstance
perpetual copulation

She hops and wiggles her ears, then waits
for the male to recuperate.

He, king of the lipsticks,
emits a long ultrasonic whistle.

She stretches on the floor for a doze.
He just grooms himself quietly.

Honeysuckle, underwear in the moonlight.

Underwear in the Moonlight Sonata

minimalist period

slow lorises, black langurs

A two-hundred-ton merchant ship called **THE FETUS.**

"I remember Mama."

Long years of grey service.

The pudding in its crypt.

Her enormous summons.
                            Lifelong
nostalgia for cryptology.

A visit to the dome
of our next teapot.

        Double-jointedness as a child
recalled by Mrs. Maple,
first grade teacher.

(Mrs. M.:)

He was a quiet child. He was a quiet,
well-behaved child. He was a thoughtful
child who like to read books. He was a quiet,
well-manicured, thoughtful child who liked
nothing so much as to curl up with a good book.
He was a well-behaved, well-manicured child
who like to curl up quietly with a book.
He was so quiet we thought he was dim. He
was a quiet...

        Oral Sunday
and may the best church win.

□□■□□

(Photo-Montage:)

    Do-It-Yourself Conspiracy

blackgum, sourwood

(Ten seconds in, VO:)

The study turned up some not-so-
surprising things, such as that
people are three times more likely
to feel lonely when alone.
                    It also found
people alone less self-conscious, better
able to concentrate,
less happy and more irritable,
bored and sad.
              More significantly,

Hammurabiphobia,
a malady of cats.
              Irresistable
propensity for running away.

other research has shown that
adolescents who spend more time
alone show greater purposiveness
and direction in their lives.

Whipping it out of them.

stinkweed, stickyheads, bladdernuts,
soapwort

(Headline:)

FAMILY JULES BECOME AUTOMECHANIC

Why not two ewes?   "Why not two ewes?"

Destruction of the mukluks.

(VO:)

Charging 15¢ per guinea pig, it took
The Conspiracy three years to retire
the mortgage on its kangaroo.

A biological freshman.

The veracity of toads,
two Rutgers University professors think.
A pimple in your heart.

The Conspiracy constructs an amoeba
from out of ammonia and gunpowder.

A logical freshman.

(VO:)

If behavior modification is any
indication of intelligence, toads
are the most intelligent amphibians.

(VO:)

He's a florist, so he knows all about life.

Common cement. Mortarboards.

(CU:)

A bucket of holes.

"common sewer of erudition…bastard of arts
…bogus hope…gold-plated syringe…
the live-in genius…exaggeration to the world."

Jellyfish Rag

□□■□□

zen violence

Navy lieutenant
at the Battle of Twiss.
Toe-nail poisoning.

Out of the jungle
feeling just like Davy Crockett.

"Nothing good comes easy."

INTROMISSION: RISE and BE SEATED

The Conspiracy achieves Congress.

"Excuse me."
"Certainly."
"Our first lay in eight months."

(Tight Two-Shot:)

The Conspiracy's gross national happiness.

Boring Spech No. 12. (In ten seconds
we compress the three hours of activity
required to fill and empty the Rotunda
and deliver the meringue.)

The Conspiracy agrees.
The Conspiracy disagrees.
The Conspiracy agrees but
offers a friendly commandment.

Conspiracy relaxing around the carpool.
Conspiracy surprised. Conspiracy
absolutely deflated by this subdivision.
Conspiracy bored by the same ole cottage cheese.

(Freeze Frame:)

Between The Porch and The Tub

(Supertitle:)

time to bleed the turkey

Symbiotic Saprophytes (pianissimo)

(Group Chromo:)

      The Supreme Complicity
      on the winter steppes

Conspiracy surpliced.

Symbiotic Saprophytes (triple pianissimo, una corda)

(CU:)

Conspiracy shooting its cuffs.

Symbiotic Saprophytes (piano accordian)

(Supertitle:)

Time To Bleed The Turkey

Symbiotic Saprophytes (piano wire)

Cholmondeley and Featherstonehaugh Conspiracy
in England.

□□■□□

Wipe to Deputy Leader of the Free World
down to one sock and a truss.
Police suspect
irregularities in Jesus movement.

mosquitoes, misquotes

(VO:)
Time to bleed the turkey.

The Conspiracy winds its watch.

□□■□□

Interviewed at the Potash Works of Sodom.

on etiquette   ''The polite approach is how
I was brought up in life.
I don't kow-kow. I don't grubble.
I treat them like you treat a waiter.''

on The Conspiracy's minimalist period   ''Light reading for heavy breathers.''

on marksmanship   ''The ability
to keep the pistol on for the rest of your life
is a function of the holster.''

on survival in the wilderness   ''I against my brother, my brother
and I against our cousin, my brother
and I and our cousin against the world.''

on orderly transition   ''First
somabitch the captol
is Sultan.''

on the minimalist period   ''.''

The Conspiracy does not enjoy the interview.

□□■□□

(Zoom into headline:)

CONSPIRACY MISSING THREE MONTHS

Deputy Leader of the Free World
hard-eyed at camera.

gibbous gibbering

"I will not be a party
to a forlorn hope party."

mud (sotto voce)

The Conspiracy, missing six months,
sends its regrets.

harmonic tremors

tephra, pyroclastic material

Tephra, pyroclastic material.

(Strobing Supertitle:)

TIME TO BLEED THE TURKEY

MAGMA CHAMBER

MAGMA CHAMBER

MAGMA CHAMBER

□□■□□

Right in the middle of his solo.

                        Shot four times
in the head of the family. Nose collapses.
Police suspect orgy of punctuation.

Notably Not Able (2/4 time)

Male's post-ejaculatory whistle
a message to "take it easy."
Two Princeton University professors think.

(Wide Pan:)

      The Bay of Condolence, where
all the bad passions of the disappointed
sit like ~~crows~~, and we   cows
console our friends, if plucked
and left at a non-plus.

walking gobbies

walking serpent heads

creeping jesus

walking blennies

In the tear garden.

''There is nothing more useless than an unloaded gun.''

A decent interval.

(Headline:)

THE TESTICLES CHANGE PLACES
BUT THE SHARK GOES ON
POPE REMAINS BULLISH ON AMERICA

(Establishing Shot:)

The White Hearse.

(Evening News Voice:)

The Conspiracy is reported to have rented the entire top floor of heaven.

The First Doily.
The Gargoyles and their Hobbies.

□□■□□

Terrific view of the maul.

Among the Parsley (Part I)

□□■□□

On the dais, horizontal pupils
with gold and silver irises.

Gog and Magog agog.

Sloath of Office rears its head.

(Evening News Voice:)

In its inception speech
The Conspiracy washes its hands forever.

symbols, tiffanies, busboys

□□■□□

I–We

"I think We see what I believe. I see
what We know and We know I will see
what We think I will wish. This pledge."

Slight of hearing.

(Open mike picks up Chief Petty
Officer in the bridge:)

                "The opera isn't over
until the fat lady sings."

□□■□□

ectoplasm

(CU:)

    Ectoplasm.

(VO:)

A one word president.

woof-woof   *arf-arf*   **BOW-WOW**

wau-wau

wang-wang

oua-oua

gau·gau

wan-wan terre-terre

ham-ham   *su-su*

HOW-HOW   *su-su*   *su-su*

sum-sum   *bzz-bzz*

kʀí-kʀí   **rou-rou**

ri-ri

Miaou-Miaou   hi-han

meuh-meuh

tou-tou

BROU·HA·HA

A prisoner of eulogies.

Innocuous bi-standers.
Ben-herded.

applesauce

□□■□□

The First Hounded Daze

Interrational situation.
Economic dun-cow. Condition white,
servile deference. Reification centers.
Petrified sacred quagmires. Microphone hats.
Ancestor worshippers carrying ivory, cases
of child destruction, a pig of Galena lead.
Big bucks in pilgrimage.

Pornographic relish.
Libido. Thinking. Medical police. The very
conscience of capitalism. Selling urine
to the urinal. Unending Battle of the
Three Stools. Pettifogging economy of candles.
Mobilizing the pigeons. Escargots sympathiques.

The scratching on the wall.
Troublesome Creeks. In front of the front.

Polka Dot Politburo (jujube)

''Never mind, it will happen tomorrow.''

''The elephants are making a pest of themselves.''

Pellegra for Dinner (lento)

''Go and eat soap (et cetera)...''
''Stick 'em with a fork (et cetera)...''

Flying Coffins

''If they did not exist, it would not

Tangible slogans. Less than the standing grain.
Last rights. Lost rites. Lost rightists.
Six hundred thousand years on earth. Administrative
carapace. Stereo types. Video cassette types.

     Salting the pâté de foie gras. What a faux pas!
Dabbling in blue chip art. Spending Mother's
wooden leg in Reno. Rows and rows of country
pumpkins. Temporarily damaged by miracles.

                 Urban renewal.
Cessation of all bombing below 82nd Street.
Navel brocade. Up to their necks
in the retina. A wash on an oily sea.
Grandma's extorter chewing oakum. Shedding
a tear for Nero.

        The cow gives dividends.
The duty-free duty to be free. Escape
from a ruptured skull. The circus rampant.
The layer cake absolute.

Rin-Tin-Tinabulation of the bells.

be necessary to ignore them.''

"Better a bad joke than no joke."

"What are these old cows so cross about?"

Centipede Waltz

"Everybody dances. This is democracy."

(CU, Telegram:)

**CONGRATULATIONS
ON RESTORING ORDER IN BOHEMIA STOP**

(VO:)
In many cases, the events were wrong.

□□■□□

Insectivorous observers.   *morbid enlargements, fatty degenerations*

Minister of Rites.
Grand Chamberlain.
Keeper of the Eunuchs.
Minister of Dainty Pleasures.

permanent giggle

The most murderous room in the house.

"What can we do to convince you we love you?"
"You have only to love us and we
will no longer doubt it."

□□■□□

(Wide Pan:)
       Arrival from Houston
by Lear Jet.

hubbub

(CU, Tee-Shirt:)

Conspiracies visit exotic places
meet interesting people
and kill them

Offered a hat. Resists.

"We never wear a hat."

□□■□□

Culture.   *pas de deux*

                                               (Conspicuous duration.)

                                               ''Why not two ewes?''
                                               ''Why not two pots of dew?''

□□■□□

kiddie litter

Greeting school children.
                    Lifelong
nostalgia for cryptology.
Fingernail inspection.

The Phantom School Bus

Meanwhile, Bach at the reunion.

(Reaction Shots:)

          Rolex watches

    gold good-luck buddhas
                four-color

         tattoes, centerfolds

blond ladies

       completely iced with

           diamonds

Among the Parsley (Part II)

''If we're fighting in Buddha country
we talk to Buddha.''
                ''We don't jump off tables.''
''We'd probably be in jail if we weren't
specially trained heroes.''
              ''we rarely sing
in the morning.''
        ''9936 insects in 122 days.''
''When you bake a cake some of the flowers
stick to your thumbs.''
             ''We don't shoot
anything that can't shoot back.''
          ''We research
our food, we eat anything that's moving.''
             ''Heaven
is very expensive.''

saxophone break

The Conspiracy's stoical philosophy.   ''The universe is web-footed and enmeshed.''

ENCYCLOPEDIA BRITANNICA sinks. The eye
that looked human was glass.

Aged in the casket.

What proof?

□□■□□

Overcome with calligraphy.

(CU:)

ALGEBRA, SOLID GEOMETRY, CALCULUS & POLIO:

**DO GOD PERSIST AND
ARE HE MORALLY WE?**

lace & ruching in the tear garden

(segue) *Summa Conspiratio*

turkey malaria (triple pianissimo)

□□■□□

Artful Stimulants (galoshes, tuba)

Tipsy on its fourth martini.

(Dolly In, Dolly Out:)
Dukes, butlers, and people who think
the word ''Abramowicz'' a joke in itself.

(VO:)
But the apocalypse had to be postponed.

□□■□□

ENCYCLOPEDIA BRITANNICA sinks.

ENCYCLOPEDIA BRITANNICA sinks.

ENCYCLOPEDIA BRITANNICA sinks.

Removal from office by depilatory.

Sympathetical mummies.

half an aspirin of sperm
a gallon of eggs

□□■□□

Empty vacuum.

(Dictionary Voice:)

a combination or
an agreement between
two or more
persons formed for
accomplishing an un-
lawful end or a
lawful end by un-
lawful means. Or
in other words

Parturition & traumata: vitamins (et cetera)

newt music

INTROMISSION: RISE and BE SEATED

Heir in the Moonlight

The besotted infant in its crypt.
False teeth under a pillow.

(very small voice:)
"Why not two ewes?"

Beethovean Silence

Filmed on location at The Conspiracy

Produced and Directed by

After the novel by

Screen adaptation by

Associate Producer

Cast
(in order of appearance:)

Empty Vacuum
Dictionary Voice
Black's Dictionary of Law
Parturition & Traumata
Vitamins
a, e, i, o, and u
Marble Sonnets
Prose Before Swine
Newt Music
Voice Over
Ladies and Gents
National Anthem
The Conspiracy
Pump & Circumstance
Perpetual Copulation
She
He
Underwear in the Moonlight
Honeysuckle

Mukluks
Guinea Pigs
Kangaroo
Biological Freshman
Toads
Rutgers University
Amoeba
Florist
Logical Freshman
Common Cement
Mortarboards
Erudition
Bastard
Genius
Jellyfish
Bucket of Holes
Zen Violence
Lieutenant
Toenail
Jungle
Davy Crockett
Congress
Gross National Happiness